A Kid's Guide to Martial Arts

JUDO

柔道

Alix Wood

PowerKiDS press

New York

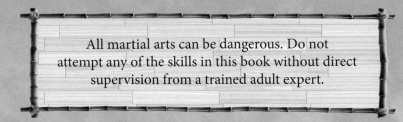

All martial arts can be dangerous. Do not attempt any of the skills in this book without direct supervision from a trained adult expert.

Published in 2013 by The Rosen Publishing Group, Inc.
29 East 21st Street, New York, NY 10010

Editor: Sara Antill
Designer: Alix Wood
Consultant: Sandra Beale-Ellis, National Association of Karate and Martial Art Schools (NAKMAS)

With grateful thanks to Finnian Cooling and everyone at Kernow Martial Arts; James, Joshua, and Elaine Latus, Olivia and Dereka Antonio, Solomon Brown, Ryan Fletcher, Alex Gobbitt, Hayden Hambly, Max Keeling, Joshua Nowell, Kyanna and Katie-Marie Orchard, Natasha Shear, Niamh Stephen, Chris Tanner, Jazmine Watkins, and Emily.

Photo Credits: Cover, 1, 2, 5, 6, 7, 8, 9 right, 10, 13 top left, center, and right, 18, 19, 29 top, 31 © Shutterstock; 3 © istock; 25 © Fotolia; all other images © Chris Robbins

Library of Congress Cataloging-in-Publication Data

Wood, Alix.
 Judo / by Alix Wood.
    p. cm. — (A kid's guide to martial arts)
 Includes index.
 ISBN 978-1-4777-0318-2 (library binding) — ISBN 978-1-4777-0358-8 (pbk.) —
 ISBN 978-1-4777-0359-5 (6-pack)
 1. Judo—Juvenile literature. I. Title.
 GV1114.W653 2013
 796.815'2—dc23

                              2012035220

Manufactured in the United States of America

CPSIA Compliance Information: Batch #: W13PK2: For Further Information contact Rosen Publishing, New York, New York at 1-800-237-9932

Contents

What Is Judo? 4

The History of Judo....................6

Judo Equipment..........................8

The Dojo 10

Warming Up..................................12

Postures and Grip 14

Learning to Fall..........................16

Balance, and Breaking It..........18

Reaping and Sweeping 20

Hip Throws 22

Shoulder Throws........................24

Groundwork 26

Competitions 28

Glossary 30

Websites 31

Read More 32

Index...................................32

What Is Judo?

*Judo is a martial art that started in Japan. Judo uses balance, quick movements, and **leverage** to beat an opponent. A small person can beat a much larger one once he or she has mastered these skills.*

Judo is a very popular martial art. It is practiced by millions of people all over the world. Judo is taught in schools in many European and Asian countries. People practice judo to stay in shape, develop self-confidence, learn self-defense, and so that they can enter judo competitions.

Most of all, people practice judo to have fun!

OLYMPIC SPORT

Judo is now an Olympic sport. It was first included in the Summer Olympic Games in 1964 in Tokyo. Only men took part at first. Women were first awarded medals in 1992.

Judo is character-building. Hundreds of hours of practice will soften any hard edges a person's character may have! After hours on the mat, you learn that the powerful can be overpowered, the overpowered can get powerful, students can become teachers, and teachers can still learn. You learn how to get up when you're beaten, take victory humbly, have **empathy** for the weak, and have respect for the strong.

The History of Judo

Judo was invented in 1882 by Jigoro Kano. At the time in Japan, a martial art called jujitsu was popular. Kano was a black belt in jujitsu, but wanted to create a style that was less brutal.

Jigoro Kano first learned jujitsu because he was being bullied at school. At age 14 he was sent to a boarding school. He was very small for his age and wanted to learn to stand up for himself. Judo uses techniques Kano had learned from jujitsu, but unlike jujitsu, judo has no strikes and doesn't use weapons. Judo uses mostly wrestling-like moves instead. The name "judo" means "gentle way."

JAPAN

● Tokyo

Jigoro Kano's first judo school was in Tokyo, Japan.

Map of Japan

A TOUGH TEST

In 1886, a few years after judo was invented, the Tokyo police held a contest between judo and jujitsu fighters. There were 15 fights. The judo fighters drew two and won the other 13!

The symbols say "ju" on the left and "do" on the right.

The emblem to the left is often used at judo schools. The design is said to look like a cherry blossom. The cherry blossom was an important symbol for the **samurai** because at the height of its beauty, it dies. The samurai were fierce Japanese warriors who practiced martial arts. Samurai had to be willing to die in their prime, too. The emblem also represents a piece of red hot iron surrounded by pure white silk, hard in the center, soft on the outside, showing that gentleness can control force.

Judo Equipment

To practice judo safely you will need special clothes. It is best to buy your kit from your club to make sure you get the right type. At first, wear loose clothing like sweatpants and a T-shirt.

The suit you wear for judo is called a **gi**. A gi is usually white pants and a white jacket, tied up with a belt. The jacket and pants are made from tough material, so they do not rip. In contests, one of the fighters will wear a different colored gi so the judges can tell the two apart.

The gi's cuffs and lapels are stitched to strengthen the material.

How to tie the belt

Place the middle of the belt on your stomach.

Pass each end of the belt behind you and back to the front.

Cross the right end over the left end.

Thread the same end up behind both loops.

Cross the left end over the right end. Thread the left end back through the hole to finish the knot.

Judo belt colors usually follows the order below, but it can vary. You will start with a white belt.

White	12th kyu
Yellow	11th kyu
Orange	9th kyu 10th kyu
Green	7th kyu 8th kyu
Blue	5th kyu 6th kyu
Purple	3rd kyu 4th kyu
Brown	1st kyu 2nd kyu
Black	1st dan to 5th dan

Some schools also have striped belts in between the levels, like the boy on page 4 is wearing.

9

The Dojo

The place where you learn judo is called a **dojo**. The dojo can be a multipurpose hall or a specially-built martial arts school. Dojos will usually have some rules and **etiquette** you must learn, like bowing.

The bow, called a "rei," is an act of respect. It is also done for safety. The first bow, done with the whole class and instructor, focuses the class on judo. The instructor also has a chance to check that students have removed any jewelry and are clean and tidy. Then you bow at the beginning and end of working with a partner. The first bow shows you are ready and the second shows you have finished and will no longer attack.

Someone who practices judo is called a judoka. This judoka waits patiently for his turn on the mat.

SAFETY IN THE DOJO

- Do not wear a watch or jewelry.
- Keep your fingernails and toenails short.
- Tie back long hair with a soft hair tie, not anything metal.
- If you wear glasses, you can get prescription goggles for martial arts. Most people try taking their glasses off to start with.

What should this boy do to be safer in the dojo?

Your instructor is called a **sensei**. He will show you how to learn judo safely. Discipline is important. Judoka must listen carefully to their sensei and try hard to follow his advice.

Judo mats are called tatami.

Warming Up

It is important to warm up before you start your judo session. Warming up stops you from pulling muscles. If you feel any pain, stop and switch to another exercise or stretch. Don't strain anything.

Thigh stretches

Lift up one leg behind you. Hold onto your foot. Gently lift your foot up and behind you until you feel a stretch along the front of you thigh.

Arm circles

With your arms out at your sides, make small circles **clockwise** and then **counterclockwise**.

Neck circles

Move your head around in a big circle. Look up, to the left, down, and to the right, and then try going the other way around.

Touch the floor

Stand with your feet wide apart. Raise your hands above your head.

BREATHE

Take deep breaths while you stretch to let your muscles relax. If you hold your breath the stretches don't work as well.

Slowly bend down and touch the floor. Try with fingertips first, then with flat hands.

If you can, try it again with your feet together.

Postures and Grip

Posture is very important in judo. Good balance is vital. You also need a good, strong grip to hold on to your opponents and stop them from falling away from you.

Basic natural posture *(Shizen-hon-tai)*

Stand naturally with your feet spread slightly apart and toes pointing outward. Relax your knees, keep your back straight, and keep your eyes level.

Right natural posture *(Migi shizentai)*

Same as the basic posture, but here the right foot is forward slightly.

Left natural posture *(Hidari shizentai)*

Same as the basic posture, but the left foot is forward slightly.

Basic defensive posture *(Jigotai)*

A low crouch with legs wide apart, knees bent outward, and body leaning slightly forward. It's a defensive position and makes it difficult for an opponent to throw you.

Right defensive posture (Migi jigotai)

Left defensive posture (Hidari jigotai)

Standard judo grip

Grip your opponent's lapel with your right hand. This grip is called *tsurite*. Grip her sleeve under the elbow with your left hand. This grip is called *hikite*.

This grip is good for both attack and defense. Hikite means your pulling hand and tsurite means your lifting hand.

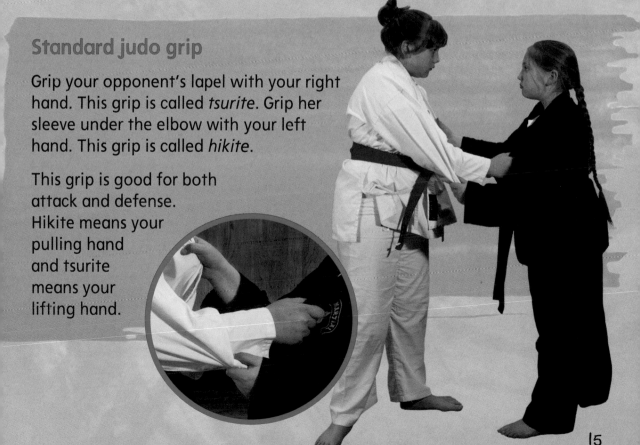

Learning to Fall

Judo uses a lot of throws. You need to learn to fall safely and get back up to protect yourself as quickly as possible.

Here are some simple breakfalls to get you started. Do them on a soft surface so you don't hurt yourself.

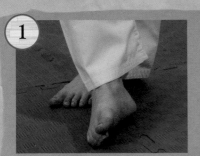

1

Side breakfall

Stand with your feet level. Place your right foot in front and to the left of your left foot. Rest the side of your foot on the floor.

2

Let yourself fall to the right. As you land, slap your right arm on the floor.

SLAP!

The harder you slap the floor, the easier you land! It spreads your weight out better, stops you from landing on your elbows, and it cancels out a lot of the force of landing. The more of your body that hits the floor at once, the less force is on one area.

Back Breakfall

From the standing position crouch down and cross your arms over your chest. Be sure to also tuck your chin into your chest.

Now fall onto your back, throwing your arms out to the side to break the fall. If an attacker is in front of you, you may want to strike by thrusting your legs to the front.

Forward roll

Use a mat to practice your forward roll. This roll can be a breakfall or an escape.

1 With your right foot in front of your left, drop your right arm toward your left leg and tuck your chin into your chest.

2 Roll forward along your right arm and shoulder.

3 Come up on your right foot and twist into your ready stance. Face the direction you just came from.

17

Balance, and Breaking It

What is balance? Is it a good stable posture? Balance is also the harmony between mind and body. A good judoka will not only try to unbalance his opponent physically, but also mentally.

Balance

To keep balance, keep your center of gravity inside a small imaginary circle drawn around your feet. To break your opponent's balance, get his center of gravity outside that circle.

CENTER OF GRAVITY

The center of gravity is the center of an object's weight. If you were balancing on a pole and started to wobble forward, your center of gravity would have gone forward, too, and you would be off-balance.

A judoka is off-balance when he attacks and when he defends. When your opponent comes toward you, you can pull him off balance. When he backs away, you can push him.

Leverage is important, too. It is easier to lift a heavy object if you put a crowbar under it. That's leverage. When you push your opponent backward, put your leg behind his leg. Your leg acts like a lever and he will slam to the floor.

Breaking balance

Breaking balance is called *kuzushi*. One of the best ways to get your opponent off-balance is to push or pull the opposite way you actually want him to go. As you push, he will resist by leaning his full weight toward you, then it is easy to pull him down using his force as well as your own.

LEVERAGE

Of course leverage applies to throws. But did you know it applies to grips, too? The wider your hands are apart, the greater leverage you have over your opponent.

Reaping and Sweeping

Reapings throws and sweeping moves aim to sweep your opponent off his feet. You can use your legs, feet, or even your hands.

Leg reap

1

2

Grip your opponent. Pull her toward you, then change direction and push her back. Hook your right leg around her right leg.

Keep hold of your opponent as she falls so she can't escape.

When your opponent tries the leg reap, step back with your left foot and lean forward. Then you can throw him instead.

Foot sweep

1

Grip your opponent and pull her forward and to her right. Stop her from moving her right foot by slapping into it with your left foot.

2

As you pull her forward she will become off-balance and fall.

Counter to footsweep

1

As your opponent slaps her foot on your ankle, quickly lift your right foot (step 2) so your opponent's foot passes underneath.

2

3

Sweep her leg to the side.

21

Hip Throws

You need timing and the strength of your hips and your legs to do a good hip throw. You shouldn't need your arm at all except to hold your opponent in position.

Large hip throw

Grip your opponent's belt with your right hand. Turn so that your back faces your opponent.

Push your hip against her and grip to lock her in position. Bend your knees.

Straighten your legs and lift your opponent over your hip. She will fall to the mat.

Floating hip throw

1 Put your right foot just inside your opponent's right foot. Place your other foot so your feet are wide apart.

COUNTER

Counter a floating hip by quickly sweeping your attacker's foot as he steps across to do the throw.

2 Turn so your back faces your opponent. Quickly bring your left foot in by your right foot, which will lift your opponent up onto your hip.

3

4 Keep hold of his wrist so you can follow with groundwork.

Turn your hips to the left. This will throw your opponent onto the mat.

Shoulder Throws

When performing a shoulder throw, you need to get down low, so bend your knees. The power comes when you straighten your legs. You will need to have a good grip on your opponent, too.

Shoulder throw

1 Turn your back on your opponent. Grasp her sleeve with your left hand.

2 Bring your right arm around her right arm, squeezing tight.

3 Bend your knees and bend forward, levering her over your back.

Counter to shoulder throw

1

Your opponent tries to get her right arm under your right arm.

2

Bend your knees. Move your feet apart into a wide, stable stance.

3

Straighten you knees and lift her in the air. Tip her onto her back.

What makes a good throw?

Kuzushi, controlling an opponent's balance, movement, and position.

Tsukri, the movement where the attacker fits his body into position to throw his opponent.

Kake, the actual throw.

Kime, the follow-through to the throw.

Groundwork

Groundwork is an important part of judo. You need to gain the advantage once you and your opponent are on the mat. You can use holds or leverage on a joint.

Armlocks and leverage can cause damage to **ligaments**. It is important to not apply full pressure when you are training.

Scarf hold

When your opponent has fallen, drop down on your knee and hold him down.

Lean your full weight on your opponent's chest. Wrap your arm around his neck. Hold onto his arm and pin it across your body. Spread your legs out wide.

Cross armlock

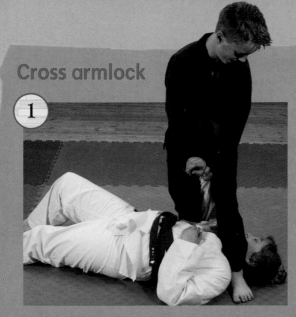

1

After a throw, keep hold of your opponent's wrist. Step over her head with your left foot. Push your right foot under her back.

2

Sit down and lean back. The armlock will put pressure on her elbow joint. Do not apply too much pressure or you could damage her elbow.

A good way to escape a hold down is by bridging. Make a bridge shape with your body by lifting your hips off the mat. In a contest the countdown stops if your back is lifted from the floor, so you have gained vital time to try and get out of the hold.

SUBMISSION

Submission is when you admit defeat. To submit, tap the floor, or your opponent, with your hand or foot. They must ease the pressure as soon as you submit.

Competitions

Competitions are a fun way of progressing in judo. You can compete with other judoka and move up the grades to earn the next belt color.

Judo contests are knockout competitions. Only the winner goes through to the next round. If you keep winning you may end up in the final.

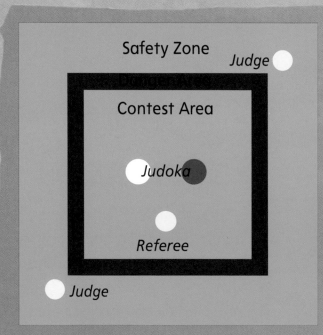

Safety Zone

Judge

Danger Area

Contest Area

Judoka

Referee

Judge

The judo tatami

Judo competitions take place on a special 26.2 foot by 26.2 foot (8 x 8 m) square tatami mat (the inner green square.) There is a danger area and an outer safety area. You must keep some part of your body inside the contest area. You must not spend more than 5 seconds in the danger zone or you will be penalized. The safety area is there to protect you if you get thrown out.

Moving up

If you beat someone with a higher belt color, you move up to that grade. Usually you fight someone in the next grade up. In this picture you can see the **referee** (far right) looking on.

When the referee invites you onto the mat, walk to the red mat area and wait. The referee will then call "rei" (bow). Bow and step forward to the center of the mat and stand on the blue or white strip. The referee will call "rei" again, and you bow again. When the referee says "*hajime*" (start) the contest begins. Keep going and don't stop unless you hear the referee call "*matte*."

Judo competitions are fun, and you may just win a medal!

29

Glossary

clockwise (KLOK-wyz)
Moving in the direction that the hands of a clock move.

counterclockwise (kown-ter-KLOK-wyz)
Moving in the opposite direction that the hands of a clock move.

dojo (DOH-joh)
A training center for the martial arts.

empathy (EM-puh-thee)
Being aware of and sharing another person's feelings, experiences, and emotions.

etiquette (EH-tih-kit)
The rules governing the proper way to behave.

gi (GEE)
A lightweight garment worn for martial arts, usually white loose-fitting pants and a white jacket.

leverage (LEH-veh-rij)
The action of a lever or the increase in force gained by using a lever.

ligaments (LIH-guh-ments)
Tough bands of tissue that hold bones together.

posture (POS-cher)
The way of holding the body.

referee (reh-fuh-REE)
A sports official usually having final authority in conducting a game.

samurai (SA-muh-ry)
A warrior serving a Japanese feudal lord and practicing a code of conduct which valued honor over life.

sensei (SEN-say)
A teacher or instructor, usually of the Japanese martial arts.

submission (sub-MIH-shun)
An act of submitting to the authority or control of another.

Websites

Due to the changing nature of Internet links, PowerKids Press has developed an online list of websites related to the subject of this book. This site is updated regularly. Please use this link to access the list:
www.powerkidslinks.com/akgma/judo/

Read More

Brown, Heather E., and Ashley Martin. *How to Improve at Judo*. New York: Crabtree Publishing, 2009.

Crossingham, John, and Bobbie Kalman. *Judo in Action*. Sports in Action. New York: Crabtree Publishing, 2006.

Mason, Paul. *Judo*. Combat Sports. North Mankato, MN: Sea-to-Sea Publications, 2010.

Index

A
armlocks 26, 27

B
balance 4, 14, 18, 19
belts 8, 9, 28, 29
bow 10, 29
breakfalls 16, 17

C
center of gravity 18
competitions 4, 28, 29

D
dojo 10, 11

G
gi 8
grips 15, 19
groundwork 26, 27

H
hip throws 22, 23

J
jujitsu 6, 7

K
Kano, Jigoro 6

L
leverage 4, 19, 26

O
Olympics 5

P
postures 14, 15

S
safety 8, 11
samurai 7
shoulder throws 24, 25

T
Tokyo, Japan 5, 6, 7

W
warming up 12, 13